Thoughts for Life

Written by Peggy Ann Binder

© P A Binder 2016

A collection of thoughts for life written from the heart, to help and heal on our journey through life.

© Peggy Ann Binder. All rights reserved.
No parts of this publication may be reproduced, stored in a retrieval system or transmitted in any form or by means electronically, mechanically, photocopying, recording or in any other reproduction technology without the prior permission of P.A. Binder.

Acknowledgments

The author wishes to acknowledge the invaluable contribution and to thank Orb Community Arts, particularly Matt, Andy and Elizabeth, for helping with the preparation of putting this book together, including the audio version. Also my son Omar, and Kathryn, for getting it to publication.

To help capture the imagination and lift your heart. Being a person of faith, I trust in God's love, which has helped me through some of the most difficult times in life. I would love to share with you some of my inspirational thoughts on my own personal experiences, to encourage, bring comfort, love and hope on your journey. I would love to share some of the happier times too. I have expressed some of my feelings on laughter, the beauty of nature, love, joy, family, life and loved ones who have passed over. I have also included in my work some of my expressions of love during recent times following the loss of my dear grandson Samuel, who was taken from us on October 2014.

A Dedication With Love

In memory of my dear Grandson Samuel who was taken

from us in 2014,

My beloved parents Derwent and Joan,

And my brother Peter who has also passed over.

They are greatly missed.

Until we meet again...

Contents

Children Playing in the Snow *p.8*
The Sound of Children's Laughter *p.10*
Evening Song *p.12*
On the River *p.13*
Spring and Easter time *p.14*
Spring Coming Through *p.16*
The Green Grass of Summer *p.17*
Winter Snow *p.19*
Winter Winter Winter Rain *p.20*
A Winter's Eve *p.21*
Mother Nature *p.23*
The Naughty Cat *p.25*
Two Grey Squirrels *p.26*
The Beautiful Robin *p.27*
Our Wedding Day *p.28*
Boyfriends *p.30*
An Angel *p.31*
A Fairy *p.32*
A Parent of Man *p.33*
The Rose a Woman *p.34*
Our Understanding Father *p.35*
Our Mother's Love *p.37*
A Mother's Point of View *p.39*
My Dear Grandson, Omar *p.42*
My Dear Grandson, Zayn *p.44*
See With Your Heart *p.46*
I Hear a Gentle Whisper *p.48*
To Walk With You *p.50*
I am With You *p.51*

© P A Binder

I Believe in You p.52
Road of Life p.53
My Lord of Grace p.54
The Will to Live p.56
God Heard and Answered p.58
I Wonder Where p.59
Life on The Other Side p.60
It Came to me in the Night p.62
A Rose (Growing by my Garden) p.64
Hello Mum (Mother's Day) p.65
Samuel, I Am Very near p.67
Christmas Robin 1 .... p.69
Christmas Robin 2 a + b p.70
Samuel, Samuel, Samuel p.72
Samuel, With Love p.73
A Place of Peace p.74
Yes Jesus is Our Saviour p.75
A Wonderland of Love p.76
If I Only Had Time p.78
Love Did Wake This Woman Me p.79
This Raging Tide p.81
Love Expressing p.83
Love at First Sight p.84
People p.85
Fashion Shops p.86
Love p.88

Children Playing in the Snow

Children running past, and out to play,
With hats and coats, and gloves and sleigh.

They're laughing and giggling (what a happy sound!)
Pulling their sledges across snowy ground.

Snowballs are thrown, and they zoom through the air,
Landing on coats, and flakes through their hair.

They're huffing and puffing with laughter and glee
As one whizzes past and lands on the tree!

Screams, out loud, with hearts full of joy,
Little children so happy, two girls and a boy!

They're meeting with others that have come out to play,
With laughter and joy on this cold winter's day.

Oh it does! It looks such fun!
I wish I could play, but my years have moved on.

Yes, my heart is still free, and I've enjoyed it too!
Just watching the children from my window-sill view.

My heart has danced, and played in the snow,
Whilst watching the children, their cheeks all aglow.

*They're running home, and their breath meets the air.
They're running, and free, and they don't have a care!*

*Yes, children run past, and they are out to play
With hats and coats, their gloves and sleigh.*

The Sound Of Children's Laughter

The sound of children's laughter ringing through the air
It really is so lovely, it echoes without care
A playful heart, a screeching sound,
Their jumping and skipping and running around.
Their childlike trust and simple ways,
A joy to watch as children play.

There's freedom and they're happy in a world that's all their own.
If we all could be like children, and that we had never really grown.
I love to play with children - in their world you're not alone.
It's fun and joy and laughter: leave adulthood at home!

They're free from all the trappings of our world of adulthood.
Of credit cards and finance, that does the heart no good.
Forever we'd be children, oh what a sight to see.
A lovely place of freedom, and real sincerity.
Lovely are the children, we can learn a lot from them.

They show the way with love and truth
Before we grow and lose our youth -
And we can't begin again.
So free your heart - be happy, as children always do.

Then you'll always hear the echo of laughter coming through.

An Evening Song!

As Evensong fills the air,
Birds settle down everywhere!
It's a beautiful sound as the light goes down;
The lamps in the street shadow the ground.
There's been a singing and an echoing
Amongst the trees,
As the birds settle down in the evening breeze.
There's lamplight now shining around,
Casting the shadows across the ground.

There are houses lit, the windows bright,
Casting the rays of luminous light.
People passing along the street,
Exchanging warm words, each other to greet.
A man walks his dog, and a car passes by;
Yes, they're heading for home, as tea-time is nigh!

© P A Binder

On The River

The River water flows with ease,
Floating past the shading trees.
Rippling water flowing along,
It's a musical sound - it's nature's song.
Rainbow colours, bright displays,
Glinting through the sunlit rays
On surface water moving along,
It ebbs and flows like in a song.
Sunlit rays caressing with ease
The surface water, passing the trees.

There are twigs and branches coming this way
As groups of children start to play.
Splashing the water - what a lovely sound,
And their laughter simply echoes around.
Ducks and chicks coming too!
Mum leads them on as they come into view.
Yellow and fluffy, oh what a sight!
Baby ducklings to give such delight.
Further along there's a bridge in view,
I can stand on the top as water comes through.
A level it drops as the lock comes in view,
And it floats round the bend, and off somewhere new.
Floating, and bobbing, and rippling along,
Yes, a musical sound - it's nature's song!

© P A Binder

Spring and Easter time!

The Meadow is green and fresh and new,
Bursting forth with life and dew.
My soul is singing, dancing high,
It's soaring upwards to the sky.
Is this a taste of Heaven?

Spring bursting forth; what a sight!
And to my eyes brings much delight.
Daffodils dancing everywhere,
Oh fresh and fragrant is the air.

As flowers permeate with ease,
They lift their heads amongst the trees
Towards the sky and sunlit rays,
Looking up as if in praise.
A natural feel about the place,
Daffodils dance, with air of grace.

Gently moving in the breeze,
All grouped around the meadow trees.
Apple blossoms everywhere!
I cannot help but stand and stare!

Birds are nesting in the trees,
Picking twigs with gentle ease,
Baby fledglings are on their way,
Whilst in their nests their eggs they lay.
There will be chirping and tweeting in the air

© P A Binder

As baby birds nestle with care.

Beaks full of grubs as mum returns,
To feed her young with grubs and worms.
A baby bird! Another song!
Easter day has come along.

What a lovely sight appears to me,
It fills my heart, and soul, with glee.
A sight of wonder, air of grace!
A sense of majesty about the place.

Baby lambs skipping around,
They're bleating for mum, what a lovely sound!
Yes, new life is everywhere!
I cannot help but stand, and stare.

Spring Coming Through

I opened up my window, oh the birds were singing clear.
It really sounds so lovely, no mistaking - Spring is here.
Just looking round my garden, it's wonderful to see
That tiny buds are growing on the branches of the trees.
There's crocus, snowdrops, and daffodils too,
There are plants and shrubs all coming through!
Spring bursting forth, it brings such delight.
New life in abundance, it's a wonderful sight

There'll be planting and sowing, digging and mowing.
There'll be weeding and raking, hoeing and staking.
Planting the borders and feeding the grass,
The pruning is done and I think it will pass.
All tidied up at the end of the day,
Back in the shed, the tools all away.
At the end of Spring, Summer will come.
It will look such a picture for the work that's been done!

© P A Binder

Green Grass of Summer

To run through the green grass of Summer
Fresh with the sweet smell of earth
Alive and filled with such freedom
A vision, the reason for living
That gave us the right to our birth.

Free as the birds in the hedgerows
As they take to the warm summer's air.
Swifts and swallows go soaring
As they drift on the thermals with care.
Birds all singing in chorus
A blackbird, a thrush and a lark,
Their music sounding so joyous
That really touches the heart.

Facing the heavens above me,
Birds all singing in tune.
Lay in a field golden with buttercups
And the warmth of the sun, mid-noon;
A picture of clouds up above me, patterns formed in the sky.
To lay here, the colours are lovely -
Watching the clouds drifting by.

To run through the green grass of Summer,
Drenched with the sun on the earth.
The flowers, their colours are lovely
To see such a vision of worth.

Bees are humming around me,
Busily working in tune
Collecting the pollen for honey
In the warmth of the sun, mid-noon.

Me, and the green grass of Summer
Free, and there's youth in my heart.
I run, I'm alive and I'm loving -
And there's nothing to keep us apart.

Winter Snow

The snow is gently falling, softly on the ground;
It looks like tiny feathers settling all around.
The sky is filled with white - it's like a duvet in the air
That's being shaken, sending feathers falling everywhere.

The ground is covered white, and it's formed a sheet of snow;
It's like a bed from Heaven everywhere you go!
It's covered all the plants and trees, and sparkles crisp and bright;
The bulbs and plants are fast asleep until new-birth, new-light.

In Spring the plants and flowers will come along to show
That winter snow was just a covering until new-life, new-buds, do grow.

Winter, Winter, Winter Rain

Winter, winter, winter rain
Tapping on my window-pane.
Go away you winter rain
Tapping on my window-pane.
Oh will the Spring flowers bloom again?
Will the flowers show their heads,
Dancing in their neat spring beds?
Will they come? I just don't know,
Amidst the bitter winter snow.
The gardens bare, an empty place
Awaiting flowers to show their face.

Winters Eve

Whilst we feel a fire's glow,
We watch the flakes of winter's snow.
And hear the touch of winter's rain
Patter on our window-pane.
And hear the breath within the breeze
Echo clearly through the trees.

A blanket, crisp and crystal white
Glows beneath the starlit night.
And in the cabin's warm embrace,
The feel of love about the place.
You and I wound as one,
And to our ears a symphony is sung.

Music moves this passioned breast,
To feel such warmth and tenderness.
I lay myself within your arms,
On overflowing to your charms.

The flames do dance and waver now,
The sheepskin rug upon the floor.
Champagne, toast and caviar.
The moonlit rays of evening light
Come streaming through the window, bright.

And on your face that warm extended smile
That gently echoes back a while.
A love so gentle, rare and free

Did reach the inner depth of we.
And you and I will want no more,
That we will see the morning come.
Alive, for love has woke, these lovers we.

Mother Nature

Can you see the beauty
That Mother Nature brings?
The leaves unfolding on the trees,
Crocus snowdrops in array,
All budding in the Spring.
A tiny bird a fledgling,
Trying out its wings.

Oh do you see the beauty,
That mother nature brings?
She brings forth life,
From Gods eternal springs.
The Wondrous beauty in a flower.
The soft cry of a bird as it takes to the air.
The gentle washing of the sea of life,
As it breaks upon the shore.
Her wonders to perform.

The rich green shades of the leaves upon the trees.
The sun drenched corn dancing in the breeze
Do you see the beauty Mother Nature brings?
To create the trees with boughs to bend
Within a breeze.
Yielding up her fruit.
Enabling man to eat from the tree of life.
She brings the kiss of life to the earth
With her tears of rain so the earth may feed
That we may survive.

© P A Binder

*She fills the earth with her wonders to perform.
Do you see the beauty Mother Nature brings?*

The Naughty Cat

I saw a grey squirrel sat on top of the fence.
Then he moved pretty fast: it didn't make sense.
I looked round the garden at what I could see -
I saw next door's cat sat under the tree.
A black and white cat, and he wasn't that thin.
I gave a load clap - he shot under the swing.
"You naughty cat!" I started to say as he's creeping along,
Frightening wildlife away.
"Go on! Go home!" Yes, I'm telling him.
He looked back at me with a scowl and a grin.
The birds and the squirrel came back in full view
As they knew next door's cat had gone somewhere new.
"I don't mind cats," I just wanted to say,
"But not in my garden searching for prey!"

© P A Binder

Two Grey Squirrels

There are two grey squirrels in my garden, in full view.
They run along the fence; they run off out of view.
They are looking for food: the acorns off the tree
Which they stored in the ground before winter came to be.
It's Spring now, and they've woken up anew
After sleeping through the Winter, somewhere out of view.
They're lovely little things - fluffy, grey and bright.
They'll wrestle with the fat balls that bring the birds delight.
They'll pull and tug, they won't give in.
Till they've got the balls and they've nipped the string.
I don't mind! I can get some more. But they will scurry back
To fill up their store.
The birds watch on, bobbing around
Looking for grubs and worms in the ground.
They'll lift up their heads, looking to see
Who's running off with their dinner and tea.
Never mind. I've got seeds, and breadcrumbs too:
The birds won't mind, neither the squirrels too.

The Beautiful Robin

Look at that robin that's sitting just there!
He's flumped up his feathers with his beak in the air.
His chest is so red as it sends out a glow,
Sitting so peacefully against the white snow.
His long skinny legs, his stockings so brown,
And his jacket of feathers all tawny and brown.

He stands very proud with his beak in the air
With his grace and such balance, as if not a care.
The robin so beautiful, a blessing to see.
Oh look now - he's flown right up in that tree!
He'll rest for a while on a branch or two.
And then off he'll go; he'll fly out of view.

He'll visit again my garden with grace
Amongst the spring flowers to sit pride of place.
What a beautiful song as his voice meets the air -
I could stand here and listen in peace, without care.
The Robin!

Our Wedding Day

The organ struck up! Its sounds filled the air.
There were family and friends, and guests everywhere.
It was a magical sound. Loved ones came into view;
They were moving along, and filling the pews.
They all sat together in colourful rows;
They're dressed to their best in their wedding clothes.

They all went quiet as the service began.
The vicar, the groom, and yes - the best man
Stood still at the altar as notes filled the air.
The bride and the bridesmaids walked to the altar with care.
She was beautiful, elegant - a wonderful sight
As the groom looked on, and his eyes were alight.

They shone out with love, together they stood
In the church at the altar, declaring their love.
The vows were taken, the rings exchanged.
"You're now man and wife!" The vicar exclaimed.

We all moved on to the reception hall.
It was a beautiful sight and we all had a ball.
There was feasting and drinking and dancing too -
Then all went quiet, as the cake came in view.
The speeches were given with laughter and cheer,
But the best man was standing and shaking with fear.
We all gave a laugh at what was said, as the groom blushed;

He was shaking his head.

Secrets were told as the bride looked on -
It's a good job for him she took it in fun!
The party went on right into the night.
They're all worse for wear: they'll sleep well tonight.
The bride and the groom left early that day:
They were catching a plane that flew them away.
Sandy beaches, as new life begins
And they've left behind all their family and friends.
They'll stay for a while, then home they will go,
Then join with their loved ones and people they know.
Cards and presents they will unwrap and view,
And send notes of thanks as their life starts anew.

Boyfriends

"Her boyfriend's come a-calling -
What do you make of him?"
"He's kind of straight and scrawny,
Or maybe he's just slim!"
"Oh will you go and see?
He's been knocking at the door."
"I told your mother clearly: him
I want to see no more.
He's really not the kind
I wanted her to see;
I thought for her a prince:
A princess she will be."

Oh a father's view is always
Really rather slim!
When viewing all the boyfriends
His view is rather grim.
"Oh, dad!" My mother said,
Looking straight at him.
"Give the boy a chance,
Go let the young lad in.
You're making such a fuss -
There's nothing you can do.
Just like my father said,
'Oh that young lad's not for you!'
Yes I know it's parents, and a father's point of view
But if I'd have listened to my dad
I'd have never married you."

An Angel

Oh, I saw an Angel!
She was standing over there!
Oh yes, she was so vibrant;
There was gold-light in her hair.
The stars in vast array
Were dancing round her head.
I rubbed my eyes to see her,
She was standing by my bed.
Her clothes were fine and soft;
She was standing in pure light.
There really was no colour -
She was beautiful in white.

Her eyes were violet blue; she
Was smiling straight at me.
She had that kind of look,
Like I was someone that she knew!
There was a feel of warmth and love,
Of tenderness and care.
I wonder if she came in answer to my prayer.
We have a guardian angel
That most of us don't see.
I guess they're always with us, with warm sincerity.

A Fairy

I saw a little fairy -
She was sitting by the tree!
She was a tiny little thing
That most of us don't see.
They have a secret place
In our gardens - did you know?
Amongst the pretty flowers,
Where shrubs and bulbs do grow.
You very rarely see them:
They have a world that's all their own.
But they're hidden out of view
In your garden; round your home!

The Parent of Man

The tree of life is the parent of man,
The bud of the leaf is the boy - a child,
Then the rich green shades of youth,
Crisp and new as the leaf unfolds
To weather the storm of life -
The strong, firm leaf is now a man.
The leaf must now survive the test of time,
To reach the years of Autumn's colours.
Man, the leaf, must fall from the tree of life,
To return to the earth again
When Autumn's done.

The Rose A Woman

The unseen Rose is still a bud:
Tend the bud with love.
Watch the petals unfold,
The colours deep and rich,
To reach full bloom a woman.
Tend your Rose - water her with love
Or she will wilt.
The Rose responds to care;
Her petals radiate her colours.
She blooms for you!
Don't glimpse in passing -
Look at the Rose; See Her Beauty Too!

© P A Binder

Our Understanding Father

He was always understanding.
We could rely upon
His judgement and his wisdom
In all that he has done.

A Father's love is something
My words cannot express.
A kind of understanding;
An inner selflessness.
Enough he couldn't do -
He gave us all we had.
Nothing more was needed
Than the kind of love we have.

We know he's always with us
In everything we do.
His guiding hand will lead us
In all we do pursue.
Our father was a man
No other can replace;
No warmer kind expression
Was seen on any face.

In times that we were troubled,
He reached us from the grave
With that kind of love and understanding
We found new hope, new faith.

© P A Binder

We know he isn't with us
In the body and the flesh.
His spirit lives among us
With his understanding selflessness.
No deeper kind of feeling
Was a family ever loved,
Like the kind our loving father
Gave to all of us.
His tender caring love
We give to mother too,
In everything we did
And everything we do.

Our Mother's Love

Our ever-loving mother!
Our mother's love was something
My words cannot express.
A kind of caring loving,
That tender gentleness.
Enough she couldn't do -
She gave us all she had.
At times her life was happy
And at times her life was sad.

She always had the patience
With tenderness and care,
And always gave us love,
And wrapped us round with prayer.
She told us all about Jesus
To help us on our way!
She gave us hope and strength
In in a very special way.

She would cook and clean, and wash and sew,
And do everything on the go!
Ironing and gardening; other jobs too -
She'd do everything a mother would do.
More than that, she never complained;
She just muddled on and carried the strain.

Eight of us! A lot to do.
A mother's love just carried us through.

© P A Binder

New schools, new friends, as we moved along -
Dad's work not secure: no place to belong.
Money was scarce; provisions were few,
But mum did her best, and so did dad too.

There were times we had plenty,
And times not too good;
At times there was coal
And at times there was wood.
We all snuggled up at the warm fireside
On a cold winter's night: it was snowing outside.
Blankets were short so our coats would do:
They would add extra warmth to see the night through.
A warm cup of tea, and some porridge too!
Ready for school, with the bus nearly due.

Mother would check for the day up ahead -
As we'd go off to school she'd be changing the beds.
With patience and kindness, with love and care,
Our mother's love was always there.

And when hurting and sick, enough she couldn't do -
Yes our mother's love would always come through.
"Her heart was worn out," the doctors did say
When our mum left for Heaven on that November Day!
Yes, she gave all she had: a heart filled with love
And now rests in Heaven with our father above!

I think they're still here, helping us through,
As a guide and an Angel -
But just out of view.

A Mother's Point Of View

Another birthday's come and gone!
I'm sixty-four years old.
With air of grace and elegance,
"You're not that age!" I'm told.
I'm young in heart, and young in mind;
I'm kind and caring too.
I'd like to feel I've held my looks:
That's just my point of view.
I'll stop and smile and give a word
To help you through your day.
With words of fun and laughter
As we both go on our way.

I miss my children more these days,
The busy lives they live.
With work and jobs about the home,
They've precious time to give.
My daughter's young and happy,
With children of her own.
They keep her always on the move -
She's very rarely home.

I've cried a tear and shared a lot
About my life and day.
With a daughter you can say such things,
As sons are far away.
My daughter is the loving kind,
Yes, young in heart as well.

© P A Binder

She's always had a listening ear,
And warm words she can tell.
I get the chance to see her;
My grandchildren sometimes, too!
I'm blessed - three boys and a girl,
From a family point of view.

A son that lives not far away,
About twelve miles or so.
It's rare the times I see him -
He's always on the go!
He's young in heart, a smiley face,
Gives hugs and laughter too!
He's my eldest son of course;
It's a mother's point of view.
And he has a daughter and a son,
And jobs that keep him on the run.

My youngest son, I miss him too!
He's many miles away.
He's in Dubai, the Middle East,

It's not that far, he'll say.
He's young in heart, a lovely lad,
With sounds of laughter too.
He'll give a hug and hold you tight
With words that help you through.
He'll help with bills and things I need
I cannot do myself.
It's all to do with internet -
The world wide web, its wealth.
He sends a ticket via the web,

To catch a plane and say:
"I thought you need a break now mum,
Perhaps a holiday."
I'll see the boys and have a laugh -
There are two of them, you know.
They'll fill my heart with love and joy
And keep me on the go!
With cars and toys we'll play our games
Until my holiday ends.
Then I'll make my way back home
To family and friends.
I hold my children in my heart,
Their children also too!
It's just my heart you know;
It's a mother's point of view.

I'll say goodnight and rest awhile;
Some things I want to say.
I'll give them all to God in prayer
To bless them on their way.

My Dear Grandson, Omar

Omar is his name, this little one.
He's the son of my son; he's a beautiful one.
He's sensitive, bright and full of grace,
Expresses himself with an open gaze,
Responds very much to touch and praise
As you talk and play, and encourage him on.

He's thirsty to learn and a bright young one.
With patient voice, he's easily led,
He will listen intently to what's being said.
He's a mind of his own, strong character too,
With an open mind and a creative view.
He will show you the way he wants to play
When you listen and smile, and get involved in this way.

"Grandma! Grandma!" he will say,
"Come Grandma, let us play!"
With cars and planes we have such fun,
In his world of play we go on and on.
We go to the beach, we picnic too;
We fly on the planes to places new.
Imaginary places with laughter and joy
He shines with love, this dear little boy!

I wait for a visit to give him a hug,
As his eyes light up with that wonderful love.
He now has a brother - his name is Zayn,

Who I hope will share in our laughter and play.
He's a beautiful boy;
He's a lovely child of my dear son.
Two beautiful boys.
Yes, my dear grandsons!

My Dear Grandson, Zayn

New life for us has just begun -
To us a child, a baby son;
A lovely boy, a new grandson.

He has a gentle face
And eyes that shine and dance about the place.
His wide extended smile
Will melt your heart as it echoes back awhile.
His nature is gentle, soft and true,
With an innocence, his childlike view.
He is a blessing, sent from above
To hold and cherish, and share our love.
Call his name and he looks with glee,
With interest and simplicity.

He will giggle and chatter with a baby sound,
As he toddles and plays and moves around.
He will hold out his hands for a cuddle or two,
Then he'll go on and play as he looks back at you.
With a smile full of love and a heart full of joy,
Yes a dear grandson, a dear baby boy!
We will love and cherish him, and teach him with care,
As he grows to a man, with blessing and prayer.
A child filled with love, wonder and glee,
Full of laughter and joy and simplicity.

Embraces and cuddles is how it should be,
And a mother's love is necessity

© P A Binder

To show the child that he is safe,
To make him secure and give him faith.
A daddy's love is important too,
To guide through the years and bring him through.

Safe in their love is how it should be,
It's not that hard: the heart holds the key.

See with Your Heart

Did you ever give from your heart?
Did you ever really see
To touch the trees,
To touch the earth,
See the sky?
Did you ever really see the beauty in life
That comes from giving unselfishly?
If you do,
Your heart flies free.

Keeping faith with yourself in others
And knowing that when you do,
You do this with a heart that's true,
All the time keeping faith with God.
See him and know whatever he sends to you.
Always do what your heart truly tells you to do,
Even if you know you will lose.
Because you have given,
You are always nearer
To God, to Life, to Others -
When you give
With a heart that's true.

Know the beauty that comes from within.
To give is to know the true wealth of life -
You will never stand alone.
Hear the rain falling in the street, see the sun.
No matter how long it should last,

© P A Binder

The sun will always shine;
You will receive your reward in heaven.
Do unto others
As you would have them do unto you.

What will be will be.
Take time to see yourself, look within;
Share your love with others -
And maybe they too will see the beauty in life.
Remember, you will always live to see another day,
If not in this world, in the next.
Only he will know
When the time is right.

So be thankful for your life.
We are but a twinkle in the eye of life.
What you seek you will find -
True love has no boundaries;
Nor has faith
Or life.

If you see beyond,
You will always know the true meaning
Of life.

See with your heart!

I Hear A Gentle Whisper,

I hear a gentle whisper
Floating through the trees.
It's soft and warm, refreshing;
Moving on the breeze.
I feel the breath of God now -
It's always in the air.
I sense and feel his love
Around me everywhere.
It's life in great abundance!
It's daily ever new.
It's always given freely, and
It's never out of view.

A bird, a baby fledgling,
Trying out its wings.
New life is all around:
God's hand in everything.
The fields are bright and green,
And there's sunlight everywhere!
The flowers - gentle colours,
And their fragrance fills the air.
It's his hand in his creation;
It's beautiful to see.
New life is all around us -
It fills my heart with glee.
There are creepy crawlers, spiders too!
There are bugs and creatures out of view.
But everything that moves and breathes

© P A Binder

Exists with love that gently echoes through the trees.

There's movement and life everywhere -
It's in his being, and in his care.
His spirit moves across his earth:
It gives new life; it gives new birth.
Always remember, he's a breath away
When he fills your heart and you want to pray.

To Walk With You

The garden, Lord, is so beautiful;
The colours are so majestic.
And every shade to see -
What an array of beauty, and such tranquillity.
Your father's heart draws near me
As I sit between the trees.

The fragrance overwhelms me
Gently in the breeze.
The birds all sing a chorus
That echoes through the air
In the cooling of the evening,
As though in choral prayer.

Yes your father's heart is near me
As I lift my heart with praise.
May I always know your presence,
And know more of your ways.

Throughout the coming of my days,
I watch and wait, and rest and gaze.
What a place of beauty!
A real joy to the heart.

I Am With You

"I am with you through the days of old, my child
When life grows weary and grows cold

I hold your hand - feel me gently
And understand you're not alone, my child

My love surrounds you through the day
When often near I hear you pray"

Oh Lord, help me understand
That you are near, to hold my hand

"And in the warm and gentle silence, be at peace
Just let my love bring soft release

Just dry your tears upon your face
Heaven is near. I understand...

Now let all go into the Father's hands
Rest now, you are loved."

I Believe In you

I see you each night before I go to sleep;
I realise you're there.
I focus on the day that's been,
With your grace, and tender care

The Spring of day has gone,
With the warmth of summer's love.
But the tide of life flows on,
With the grace of God above.

The Road of Life

The road of life is long and winding,
I must travel on.
With you ahead to guide me,
You are my light my song.
You are the peace within me
That drives me on and on.

I used to plan the days so well,
Months ahead of me.
Striving on to reach that goal,
Of which I would achieve.
But now, where am I going -
Where will you lead me next?
I'll take each day in passing,
To reach the very next.

I see the flowers, trees and birds,
The mountains and the sky.
I'll feel the joy of love's warm kiss
As the years go by.

My Lord of Grace My Shining Star

Oh God Ye are my shining star,
That shone in Bethlehem afar.
That bright and glowing shining light
Which Mary bore that stabled night.
For rich and poor, ye came to be,
For all our sins, our saviour he.

Our Lord of peace and truth and love
Was born on earth from God above.
Heavy-laden burdened frame,
He took for us our sin and shame,
Our gain eternal life to be
When confessed our sins to thee.
He came to die for all of we,
Upon that cross at Calvary.

Our saving grace that walk with men,
And ye are now as ye were then.
Within men's souls thy spirit be,
Come suffer children unto thee.
This God of grace and beauty bright,
Glowing on through spirit light.
Lead us home that life to come,
When we will be with ye as one.

Oh saviour, Lord that be with us,
From the grace, our father, God above.
With thanks and all we are to be,

© P A Binder

We come ourselves, Lord, back to thee.

The Will to Live

When the light has gone,
You walk in darkness.
The reason for life to you
Has gone.
You feel such pain and sadness,
And life for you is hard to bear -
To feel no-one can love or care,
And in a state of much despair.

To feel the world is upside down,
While you are numb and so afraid.
No understanding can be found -
Looking for a way to begin again.
To others you appear insane.

I know this feeling that you feel;
This life to you appears unreal.
The will to live is there,
And with your life you must
Value and take care.

Fight, fight - there is a way!
Live to see another day.
Have faith; try not to be afraid -
In this world fate's plans are laid.
You've taken all you can endure;
You feel nothing matters any more.
Not even you.

© P A Binder

Read my words: it isn't true.
Someone cares just for you.

Start at the beginning.
Just one way to go,
And that is on, you know.
A day at a time you will find
The darkness goes.
Step by step, the only way -
You'll get through another day.

To a library you could go,
Or even to a picture show.
Take a bus; walk through a park
Into the light from the dark.
You'll look back one day,
And know that you are on your way.
Wonder where you've been,
And look at things you've never seen,
And see the things you've never dreamed.

There is a way to live; to see another day.
I hope these words are reaching you,
And that my thoughts will help you through.
May God bless and keep you.

© P A Binder

God Heard and Answered

You came into my life when
I needed you.
You gave me peace and hope, to know you were there.
I called out to God and he heard me,
And he sent you along to care.
Just knowing, and loving, and caring -
God heard and answered my prayers.
I called out in sheer desperation;
I'd taken all I could endure.
Nothing left to experience -
I just couldn't take anymore.
With your tender care and affection,
You brought me back into the light.
May God keep you safe and bless you,
And may my prayers see you're all right.

I Wonder Where

I wonder where I'm going;
I wonder what comes next.
To travel on life's highway, this
Never-knowing path.
I walk with hope within me -
I must strive on and on.
I know you walk beside me
Each day as I move on.
I've found a resting place, my Lord -
You guided me this way.
And now I see the light, my Lord,
To live another day.
I want to share my life, dear Lord,
With someone who will see
The way I need and love him,
And his love's returned to me.

Life on the Other Side

Please don't cry
My family dear
Oh please don't cry
Don't shed those tears!
Don't cry Mum
Because I'm still here

I've gone ahead Mum
To the other side
My life has changed
I'm happy here
Don't worry Mum
Have no fear

I know you miss me
All of you
But I'm still near
Just out of view
I'm with the loved ones
On the other side

Don't shed those tears
Oh please don't cry
Till we meet again
Just sense my smile
To ease your pain
And in a while
Your heart will lift

© P A Binder

*And you will know
You have God's gift*

*Our faith brings life
On the other side
God bless you all
Oh please don't cry!*

It Came To Me in The Night

My Prayer

*I feel a gentle presence around me through the day,
And sense a silent whisper as I settle down to pray.
"I'm here, my child: I'm listening to every word you say.
As I hold you in my heart in a very special way.*

*"Just let your tears subside, and tell me all your pain.
I know you cannot see me, but I'm with you just the same.
A broken heart you're holding - just give it all to me.
As I capture every tear-drop that drops down on your knee.*

*"Be still, my child, I'm with you; you're in my arms' embrace.
My heart entwines with yours, dear child, though you cannot see my face.
I'll heal your wounds and dry your tears; right now it cannot be.
In time, my child, a peace will come that you cannot see.*

*"Just trust me now - I'll hold your hand, the days ahead to see
That I always walk beside you, and that you're very close to me.*

© P A Binder

*One day you'll see me clearly; in Heaven that will be.
To join with all your loved ones that are also here with me."*

Inspired by your loving father, God.

Love Mum x

A Dedication to my Grandson, who passed away on 11th October 2014. Dearly missed.

A Rose!

A rose gently grew by my garden wall.
It blossomed with love, and grew very tall.
It bent its head low to the windowsill.
Its petals bloomed and stood very still.
Deep, rich and red, and fragrant too
As it opened so wide, and in full view.
A rose sent with love to let the heart know
Our loved one's with God, and the rose is aglow.
I collected its petals as it grew with such care.
It was a beautiful sight, and an answer to prayer.
It started to blossom as Sam passed away.
It opened with love on each passing day.
The rose joined with Sam on the other side -
It was a prayer and a comfort, a gift and a guide.

Thank you Lord.

Love You Sam
Grandma x

Hello Mum! Mothers' Day is here

Mothers' Day is here!
Just let your heart be happy
Because you are so dear.
Every day is special
For a mother just like you.
Yes I'm always with you in your heart,
And I'm just here out of view.

I've asked grandma to write this verse
That's sent here just to say.
I'm sending you my love
On this your special day.
To let you know you're loved so much
And you're never out of view.

Remember now my smile, dear mum,
And I'm looking right at you.
Just close your eyes and think a while
And feel me drawing near.
To kiss you softly on your cheek
And wipe away your tear.
Just enjoy your day
And tell them, all my family so dear,
I'm safe in our God's love, you know -
And I love you all so dear!

Yes enjoy your day, be happy
And before you rest your heads,

© P A Binder

Just let your hearts find peace
As you go now to your beds.
Yes, be at peace and sleep
Because you know I'm also near.
Don't let your hearts be troubled –
You know you mustn't fear.

Love always Sam.

I Am Very Near

With love from the other side

Samuel

Oh did you hear me walking
On the landing in the night?
I wanted you to hear me
But not give you a fright.
I came into your room
And sat down by your bed.
I was gently looking over you,
And kissed you on your head.

Yes I heard you gently breathing
As you were sending out your prayers.
The pain inside will lessen, mum -
God hears and loves and cares.
I saw you snuggle down
And move your pillow at your head.
I know all this is so dear, mum
As I was sitting by your bed.

I see you walk and talk,
And watch you through the day.
I see you in the chair
In the morning when you pray.
I see you bring your flowers

To a place there by my bed.
I always stay and listen
To every word you've said.

It hurts, I know; I love you very much.
I rest my hand upon you
But you cannot feel my touch.
I am with you when you're walking
As you go home on your way.
I am with you all the same mum,
Yes, any time of day.

I want my family to know
I love them just the same.
I'm sending you my love too, dear dad
To help and ease your pain.

© P A Binder

The Christmas Robin

I am the Christmas Robin
And I've come along to say
I'm visiting your garden
In a very special way!

In all of God's creation
And in Heaven they do too.
They celebrate this Christmas
And God's love sent to you!

Yes it's special too, it's Christmas!
He listens to our prayers.
I am the Christmas Robin
To let you know God cares.

Yes, Samuel's with Jesus,
And there's singing up above.
As surely as the stars do shine,
I bring you Christmas love.

I am the Christmas Robin

(second version)

I am the Christmas Robin, and I've come along to say:
I'm visiting your garden in a very special way.
The birds are Christmas carolling, as do the angels up above,
As they're singing round our Saviour, to ring out Christmas love.

In all of God's creation – and in Heaven they do too –
They celebrate this Christmas, and God's love sent to you!
We are all of us God's children, and he listens to our prayers.
It's special too! It's Christmas! God knows, and loves, and cares.

---oOo---

(Third version - combined)

*I am the Christmas Robin, and I've come along to say:
I'm visiting your garden in a very special way.
The birds are Christmas carolling, as do the angels up above,
As they're singing round our Saviour, to ring out Christmas love.*

*In all of God's creation – and in Heaven they do too –
They celebrate this Christmas, and God's love sent to you!*

*We are all of us God's children, and he listens to our prayers.
I am the Christmas Robin, to let you know God cares!
Yes, Samuel's with Jesus, and there's singing up above.
As surely as the stars do shine, I bring you Christmas love.*

Samuel, Samuel, Samuel

Such a lovely lad.
He'd warmed his family's hearts
And you'd rarely see him sad.
He'd warm your heart with laughter
As if he didn't have a care.
You'd gently hear his laughter
Ringing through the air.
And a smile that gave such glee
To all that looked upon him –
It was always there to see.

He'd always have a word to share
And move about without a care.
He'd give you all the help you'd need;
He didn't have an ounce of greed.
We'll miss you Sam, life's not the same;
It's filled our hearts with tears and pain.
Yes we'll miss you Sam, that's for sure,
'Til we meet again, through another door.

God Bless you Sam! You're a lovely lad.
You're in our hearts and our hearts are sad.
'Til we meet again, and see your smiley face.
It will be in God's time and be in God's grace.

Love from Grandma.

Samuel, With Love

You're a precious child and you brought such joy
A handsome lad, yes a lovely boy.
You were blessed with a smile and filled with love
A beautiful gift from God above.

When you smiled and laughed, your eyes danced wide.
And with a sense of fun, filled our hearts with pride.
Kind and caring were your virtues too,
And you'd give what you had with a generous view.

You were tall and slim with a positive stride
And you filled our hearts with a sense of pride.
You had plans and dreams and hopes to fulfil,
And you worked very hard with your gift and skill.

You had a beautiful heart and we'll miss you too -
Yes, you've gone back to God and you're just out of view.
We'll wait for the day to see your smiling face -
It will be in God's time and be in His grace.

We won't forget; we'll never part.
We hold you with love, deep in our hearts.

God bless you Sam,
Love Grandma x

© P A Binder

A Place of Peace

A place of peace, I rest my head
And said my prayers, and gone to bed.

Just in my dreams, away from here,
To places often far and dear.

With beaches, sandy soft and white,
Which catch the ocean's glinting light.

A paradise of sand and sea,
A haven's rest awaits for me.

Sun and sand, the gentle breeze,
Will bring my heart and mind to ease.

Yes, Jesus is Our Saviour!

Yes, Jesus is our saviour,
And it's wonderful to know
That God's love's always with us,
Everywhere we go.

Yes Samuel's with Jesus,
And he shares our saviour's love -
As do all our loved ones that have gone
To God in love.

As we celebrate this Christmas,
There's singing up above.
As surely as the stars do shine,
And fill the sky this Christmas time -
They shine our saviour's love.

A radiant star in Heaven,
Shone that Christmas night
To light the birth of Jesus,
And bring the world new sight.

Don't let your heart be troubled,
As the star shone down to say,
The father gave us Jesus
In a very special way.

© P A Binder

A Wonderland of Love!

Take hold of my hand and lead me
Through our wonderland.
Let me see your smiling face,
And hold me tight in your embrace.
To know and feel this warmth and love -
Were you sent by God above?

When I saw you dancing there
I knew it was for you I cared.
Then you looked into my eyes,
And - I saw - you realised.
As we danced upon a cloud,
I heard your heart cry out loud.
Are you a dream or are you real?
Is it true, the way I feel?!
My heart took wings - it flew to you.
It cried out loud,
"I Love You Too!"

We danced and danced through the night,
You held me close, I held you tight.
The words hello, hello, meant an awful lot, you know.
The hours flew - where did they go?!
They only seemed like seconds, though.

You took me home, we sighed a sigh -
Our first goodnight, but not goodbye.
We met again; that first embrace,

© P A Binder

The deep expression on your face -
I felt your love and you felt mine.
I knew it hadn't strayed with time.
That day was ours, we won't forget.
You'll come back I hope, because we met!

If Only I Had Time

If only I had time
To do all the things I could do.
If you would only give me the time
I would spend all my minutes and hours with you.
I'd sail on the seas to eternity
And bring back the visions for you.
I'd give you the sun in the morning;
I'd give you the moon at night.
And bathe you with love and affection
To warm you through a cold winter's night.
I'd pluck from the heavens a starlet
To brighten your every day.
To make all your days full of Summer
And keep all the Winters at bay.
If only I had time.

I'd fill every morning with laughter
To warm your heart with delight.
To care and to give you my loving
In my arms, holding you close through the night.
Oh, if only I had time.

"How much time is left to me?"
I must wonder before you go on your way.
I'll still send my love and affection,
And may the starlet I gave you
Brighten your way.
If only I had time to do all these things with you.

© P A Binder

Love Did Wake This Woman, Me

When stars had all burned out
And darkness came and blinded me,
I lost my way and couldn't see.
Anger, hope, doubt and fear.

Oh and what of love, this empty me.
Weeks, months had passed away
Feeling numb and in a daze -
The empty night had filled my gaze.

The touch of love awakened me;
Did hold me up and set me free.
A love so gentle, rare and free
Did reach the inner depth of me.
Illuminous for all to see.

And as the moon shone high above
Upon the beach we share our love.
In deep embrace, wound as one
Fulfilled our love, and to our ears the wind had sung.

We felt the tide caress the sand
And saw the stars glinting in the moonlit night
Like outstretched arms upon the sea,
And heard the wind touch our ears with sweet
surrender.

The tide of love did wash us, oh so tenderly

Whilst the waves did break upon the shore,
Yet you and I could want no more.

That I could see the dawning come alive
And love did wake this woman, ME.

This Raging Tide

This raging tide within my soul
Is reaching out to thee.
This bleeding heart is crying loud
As it echoes back to me.
An arm's embrace is empty now,
All to avail like outstretched arms
For all the world to see
This longing from the inner depth of me.

A pair of eyes, a nose, a face,
A silhouette without a place.
Many feelings mixed as one,
And yet my mind goes rambling on.
Thoughts and thoughts of endless things,
Visions, plans and shattered dreams.
Pressing on, I'll find a way
To build these dreams another day.

Patience comes so hard to me,
It's "plan and act out instantly".
Others' holding back I cannot move,
Like chains wrapped tightly hold me in a groove,
Ten months have passed and nothing's done,
My hopes, my dreams, I'm building on.
How long like this must I go on?

This standing still is killing me.
I need to build a world of strength

Around the outer shell of me.
I'll work and work, and save and save,
Until fulfilled these plans I've made.
This inner strength will never wane.
I haven't given up in vain -
I'll try and try and try again.

I've done it all not once but twice for thee,
But now's the time to build a home,
A vision from the inner depth of me.

Love Expressing

With love, expressing through this aching sadness
Filled my heart with warmth and gladness.
Our eyes are but windows to the world,
To dare to look but also see -
Within our eyes we hold the key.

The touch of love is as gentle as silence,
Every day, every hour, each precious moment.
No words were needed - love.
This love that you have brought to me,
Oh has touched my soul so tenderly.
I wonder, do you really see?
Whilst in your hands you hold the key.

Love at First Sight

Love at first sight is what I felt for you:
A love so quick, so deep and true
Did melt my heart and gave it wings,
And filled my soul with many things.
And in our eyes, the things you see -
One the lock and one the key.
To meet was this: our destiny.

What is love, I'm wondering now,
That puts you through
Such pain, and how?
If this is love, then set me free,
And give me back my sanity.
A broken heart, a stolen key -
A lock without much sanctity.

© P A Binder

People

See the people going places -
Did you ever see their faces?
Do you ever stop and stare?
All shapes and sizes - going where?!

Packages, parcels, drifting by,
Socks and shoes, shirts and ties;
Hats and coats, gloves and boots;
City agents in their suits.
Man and woman, child with toy -
Christmas time! To bring such joy.

Noisy traffic in the street;
All kinds of people you will meet.
And when the day comes to a close,
They've done their shopping, I suppose!

Fashion Shops

From nine o'clock a working day,
At fashion shops to earn your pay.
With pencils sharpened clean and neat,
The shop assistants there to greet.
The fashion there you will see,
The customers to jump with glee.

Clothes to wear with style and grace
Will bring a smile to any face.
With madam, we will take much care,
We've just the things for her to wear.
Greens and browns pinks and blues -
Lots of colours for you to use!
As you go from floor to floor,
What a treat we have in store!

There's coats and dresses, skirts and blouses,
Nighties, jumpers, shirts and trousers.
Fashion clothes, we stock the lot!
It's what you'll find inside our shop.
Don't window shop! Step inside!
We'll dress you up, and boost your pride.

The shop assistants helping there,
Will show you pretty things to wear.
And when she's found the clothes she needs,
We'll slip them in the bags with ease.
And though she's leaving by the door,

© P A Binder

She'll come back one day for more!

Love

I do feel so deep a love
A warm and tender, gentle love.
The calm, the peace, the amazement
Desire unlimited and still to be content.

The hours with you will warm me
Through the days of your absence
To need your love, but not to say,
For fear that you might take the sun away.

How I do love thee!
Share and care with me.
Love is like a candle glowing in the night.
I feel such warmth and comfort
To give so much delight.

This love that you have brought to be
Is like the warmth of summers sea
That Gently washes over me.
Please stay, don't go away.
Not yet, my love - let us see another day.

Printed in Poland
by Amazon Fulfillment
Poland Sp. z o.o., Wrocław